Music Fun Books

presents

Thirty Famous Patriotic songs

for Viola

Easy & intermediate solos
for the
Advancing Viola Player

www.musicfunbooks.com

Music Fun Books • P.O. Box 1247, Pacific Palisades, CA 90272

Table of Contents

ABOUT THE BOOK:
This book is comprised of more than thirty patriotic themes that are important for students to know. Chord changes are included for teacher provided accompaniments. Additionally, the teacher may supply dynamic, articulation and phrase markings as the teacher feels appropriate.

Amazing Grace

Traditional Melody

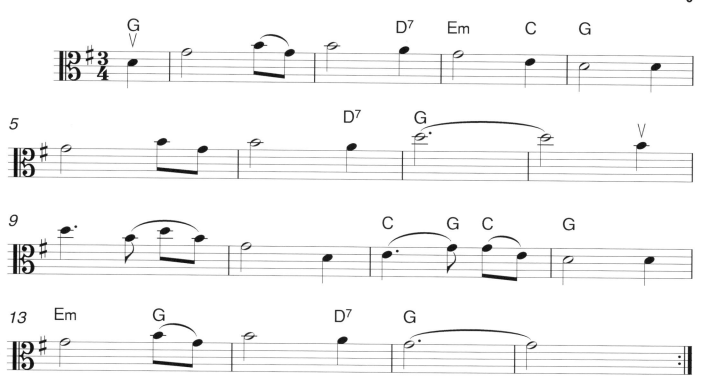

4

America

(My Country 'Tis of Thee)

M. Henry Carey

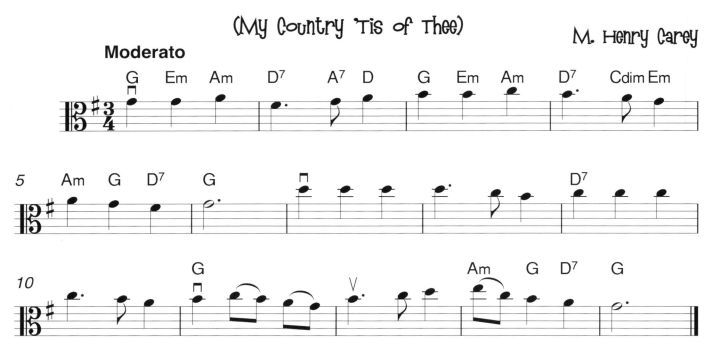

America the Beautiful

Samuel A. Ward

American Patrol

F.W. Meacham

Anchors Aweigh

The Battle Cry of Freedom

George F. Root

Moderato

Battle Hymn of the Republic

William Steffe

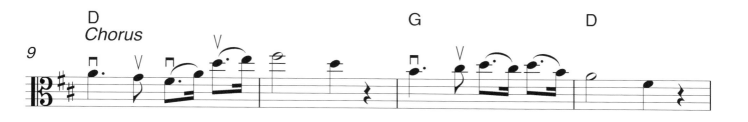

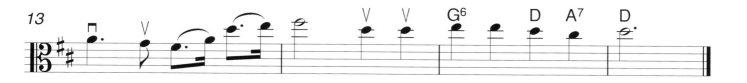

Bugle Calls

Reveille
Traditional

Taps
Traditional

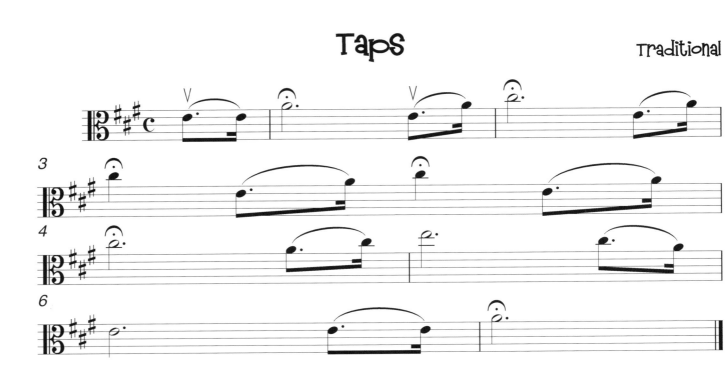

Bunker Hill

Andrew Law

Slowly, with resolve

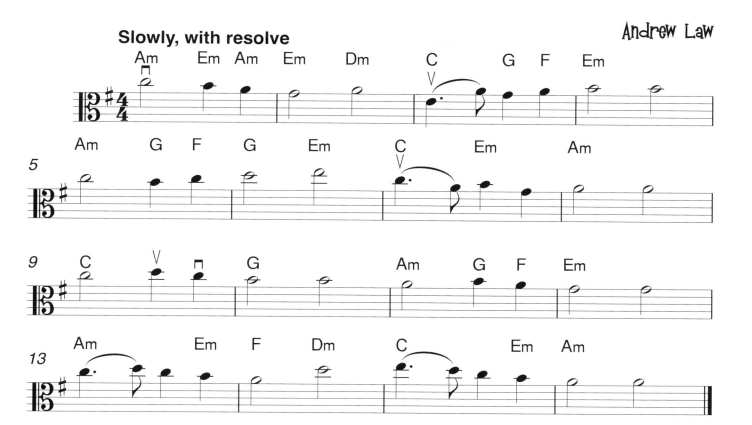

The Cassions Go Rolling Along

Edmund L. Gruber

Chester

William Billings

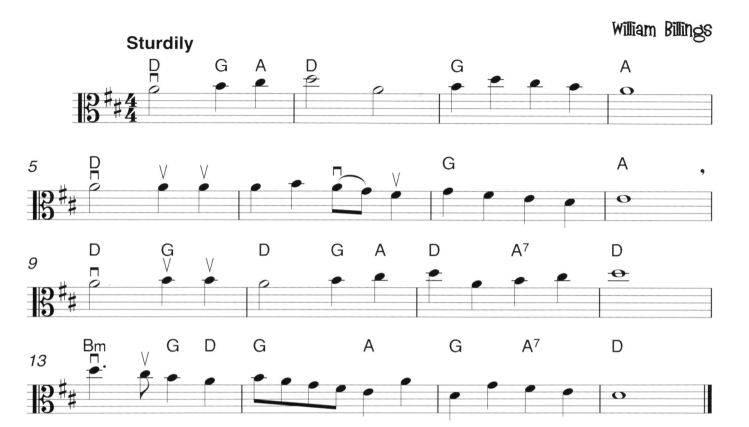

Columbia, the Gem of the Ocean

Thomas A. Becket

Moderato

Darling Nelly Gray

B. R. Hanby

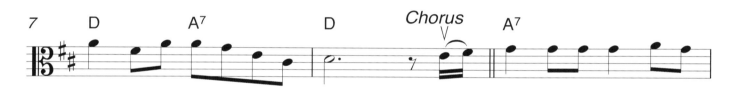

Dixie

Daniel D. Emmett

Eternal Father, strong to save

John B. Dykas

Faith of our Fathers

Henri. F. Herny

Hail, Columbia

Philip Phile

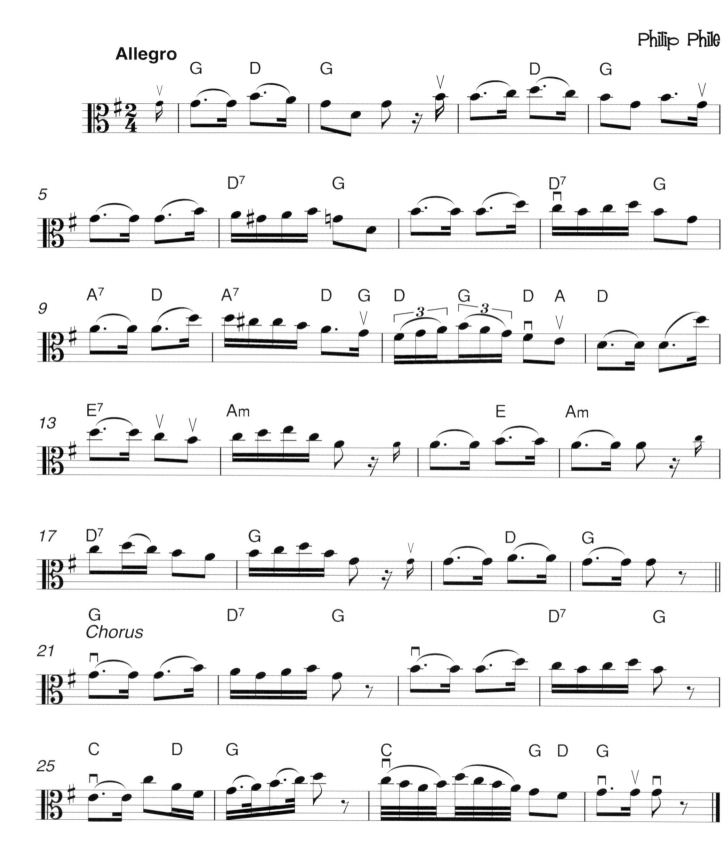

Hail to the Chief

James Sanderson

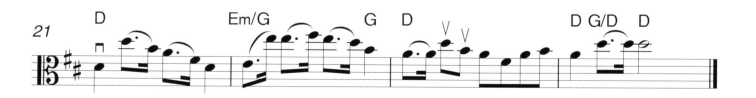

The Liberty Song

William Boyce

The Marines' Hymn

Jacques Offenbach

Maryland, My Maryland

James R. Randall

Oh! Susanna

Stephen Foster

over There

George Michael Cohan

24

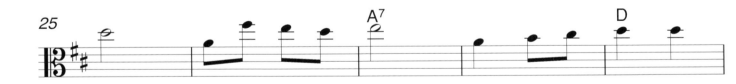

The Star Spangled Banner

With spirit, not too slow

John Stafford Smith

The stars and stripes Forever

John Philip Sousa

There'll Be a Hot Time

Theodore A. Metz

When Johnny Comes Marching Home

Patrick S. Gilmore

Yankee Doodle

Richard S. Schuckburgh

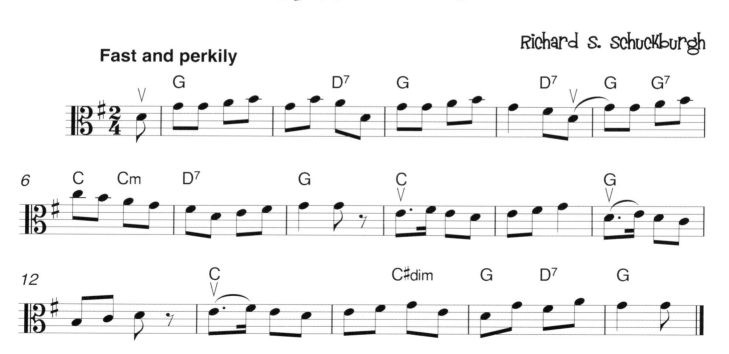

Yankee Doodle Boy

George M. Cohan

Lively March

The Yellow Rose of Texas

American Folk Melody

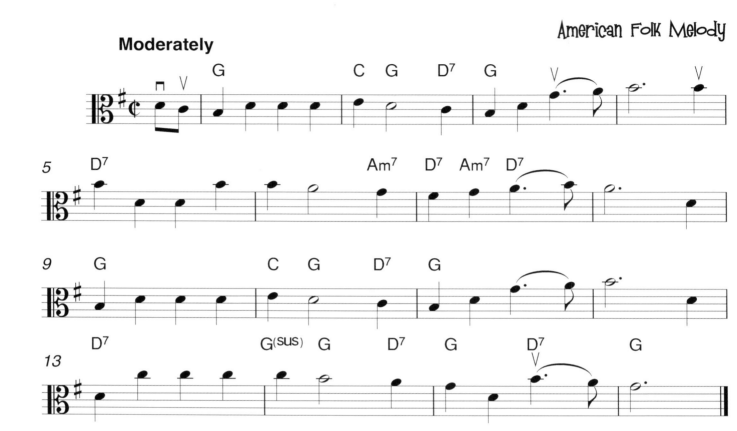

You're a Grand Old Flag

George M. Cohan

Made in United States
Troutdale, OR
01/07/2024